THE STORY OF THE
HOUSTON ROCKETS

THE NBA:
A HISTORY
OF HOOPS

THE STORY OF THE
HOUSTON
ROCKETS

NATE FRISCH

CREATIVE EDUCATION

Published by Creative Education
P.O. Box 227, Mankato, Minnesota 56002
Creative Education is an imprint of The Creative Company
www.thecreativecompany.us

Design and production by Blue Design
Art direction by Rita Marshall
Printed in the United States of America

Photographs by Corbis (Bettmann, Song Qiong/Xinhua
Press), Getty Images (Bill Baptist/NBAE, Andrew D.
Bernstein/NBAE, Vernon Biever/NBAE, Nathaniel S.
Butler/NBAE, Jim Cummins/NBAE, James Drake/Sports
Illustrated, Noah Graham/NBAE, Mark Green, John W.
McDonough/Sports Illustrated, Fernando Medina/NBAE,
Joe Murphy/NBAE, Dick Raphael/NBAE), Newscom (CNP/
Polaris, imago sportfotodienst)

Library of Congress Cataloging-in-Publication Data
Frisch, Nate.
The story of the Houston Rockets / Nate Frisch.
p. cm. — (The NBA: a history of hoops)
Includes index.
Summary: An informative narration of the Houston
Rockets professional basketball team's history from
its 1967 founding in San Diego, California, to today,
spotlighting memorable players and events.
ISBN 978-1-60818-431-6
1. Houston Rockets (Basketball team)—Juvenile literature.
I. Title.

GV885.52.H68F7558 2014
796.323'64097641411—dc23   2013038292

CCSS: RI.5.1, 2, 3, 8; RH.6-8.4, 5, 7

First Edition
9 8 7 6 5 4 3 2 1

Cover: Guard James Harden
Page 2: Forward/center Chuck Hayes (#44), guard
Courtney Lee (#5)
Pages 4–5: Guard Kevin Martin
Page 6: Center Moses Malone

TABLE OF CONTENTS

COURTSIDE STORIES

INTRODUCING...

BEGINNING LAUNCH SEQUENCE

JOHNSON SPACE CENTER HAS TRAINED AND SUPERVISED SPACE EXPLORERS FOR 50-SOME YEARS.

In the 1830s, Texas was a battleground. Mexico did not want to let go of its territory, but American settlers—called Texians—revolted. In the Battle of San Jacinto, General Sam Houston led the Texians in a definitive rout of the Mexican army and negotiated the independence of Texas. Just months later, the city of Houston broke ground a few miles from the battle site. Over time, the city's industries—shipping, railroads, and oil—thrived, and Houston grew rapidly. Today, it is America's fourth-largest city and home to the National Aeronautics and Space Administration's (NASA) Johnson Space Center—the headquarters for America's astronaut training program.

Not long after the NASA center was established in 1961, a new National Basketball Association (NBA) team was assembled in San Diego, California. The 1967 expansion team was named the Rockets, because San Diego was

home to another NASA center that developed and manufactured rockets. When the NBA franchise relocated to Houston in 1971, the club's appropriate name remained intact, and the Rockets have striven to reach new heights ever since.

In their inaugural season, the San Diego Rockets struggled to get airborne. A pair of forwards, lanky John Block and free-shooting Don Kojis, played respectably, each averaging about 20 points and 10 rebounds per game, but as a team, San Diego had nearly the poorest shooting in the league and finished with a dismal 15–67 record. The silver lining to tallying the league's worst season record was that San Diego received the top overall pick in the 1968 NBA Draft.

With that pick, the club drafted University of Houston star Elvin Hayes. The 6-foot-9 forward/center known as "Big E" gave the Rockets the thrust they needed, averaging 28.4 points and 17.1 boards per game. His size, athleticism, and determination helped him sky above the opposition to drain turnaround jumpers or battle for rebounds in the middle of a crowd. "Rebounding is a rough proposition," Hayes once noted. "But it's one of the ways I make my living, so it's something I force myself to tolerate, no

THE PUNCH

Coming off a strong playoff season, hopes were high among the Houston faithful for the 1977–78 season. On December 9, 1977, those hopes were shattered. That night, an ugly on-court fight broke out between the Los Angeles Lakers and the Rockets. It began with an altercation between Lakers center Kareem Abdul-Jabbar and Houston center Kevin Kunnert. Rockets forward Rudy Tomjanovich rushed into the melee trying to act as peacemaker when powerful 6-foot-8 Lakers forward Kermit Washington hit him with a heavy right cross. The punch was so brutal that it shattered Tomjanovich's face, nearly killing him. Although his face needed extensive reconstructive surgery and 5 months to heal, Tomjanovich made a remarkable return to the court the following year, averaging 19 points and 7.7 rebounds per game. Washington, who was suspended for two months by the NBA for the incident, still has trouble living down "The Punch." "Rudy realizes that I'm sorry, and I'm glad that he's forgiven me," Washington said years later. "Maybe when I die, they won't have on my grave, 'The guy who hit Rudy Tomjanovich.'"

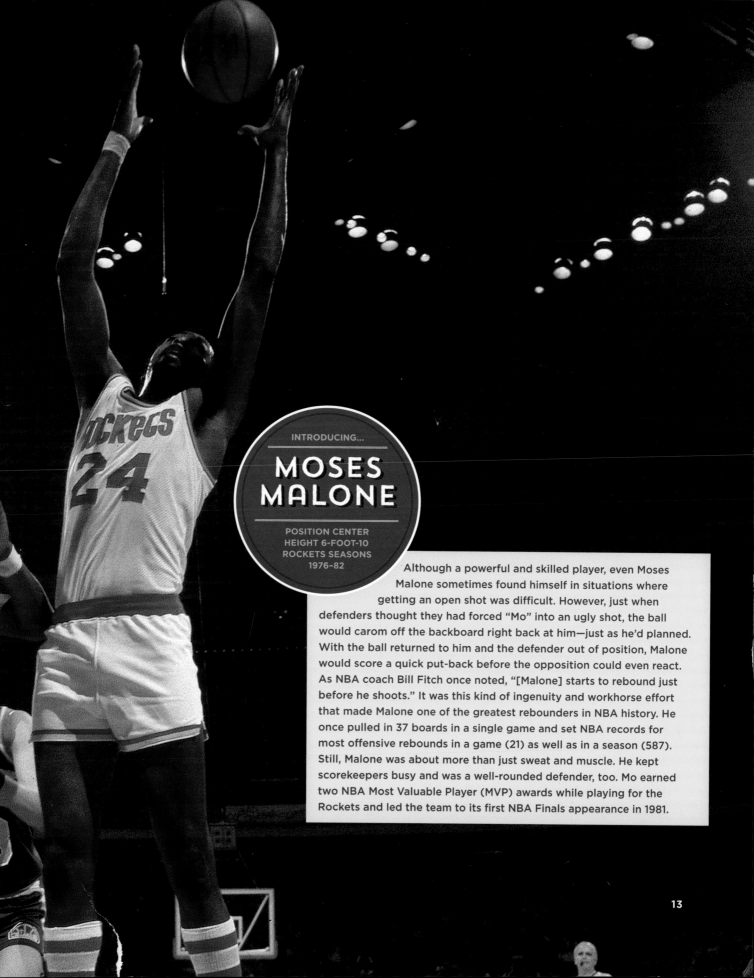

MOSES MALONE

POSITION CENTER
HEIGHT 6-FOOT-10
ROCKETS SEASONS
1976–82

Although a powerful and skilled player, even Moses Malone sometimes found himself in situations where getting an open shot was difficult. However, just when defenders thought they had forced "Mo" into an ugly shot, the ball would carom off the backboard right back at him—just as he'd planned. With the ball returned to him and the defender out of position, Malone would score a quick put-back before the opposition could even react. As NBA coach Bill Fitch once noted, "[Malone] starts to rebound just before he shoots." It was this kind of ingenuity and workhorse effort that made Malone one of the greatest rebounders in NBA history. He once pulled in 37 boards in a single game and set NBA records for most offensive rebounds in a game (21) as well as in a season (587). Still, Malone was about more than just sweat and muscle. He kept scorekeepers busy and was a well-rounded defender, too. Mo earned two NBA Most Valuable Player (MVP) awards while playing for the Rockets and led the team to its first NBA Finals appearance in 1981.

"REBOUNDING IS A ROUGH PROPOSITION, BUT IT'S ONE OF THE WAYS I MAKE MY LIVING, SO IT'S SOMETHING I FORCE MYSELF TO TOLERATE, NO MATTER HOW MANY BRUISES I WIND UP WITH."

— ELVIN HAYES ON THE HARD WORK OF REBOUNDING

matter how many bruises I wind up with."

Hayes was the franchise's first true star and the first in what would become a long line of dominating post players. He led the Rockets to their first playoff appearance after the 1968–69 season, but the team regressed the following year.

o become a legitimate threat, the Rockets needed a more balanced roster. In 1970, they drafted forward Rudy Tomjanovich and guard Calvin Murphy. The 6-foot-8 Tomjanovich offered a soft shooting touch, a knack for working the offensive boards, and a steadying presence on the court. The 5-foot-9 Murphy, meanwhile, brought lightning quickness to both ends of the court, and his accurate, high-arcing jump shots proved difficult for even the tallest opponents to defend.

Led by Hayes, Murphy, and Tomjanovich, the Rockets improved to 40–42 in 1970–71. However, low fan attendance prompted the team's owners to move the franchise to Houston in 1971. After the club's record worsened in the 1971–72 campaign, the Rockets traded Hayes to the Baltimore Bullets for

versatile swingman Jack Marin.

Hayes's departure put a dent in the Rockets' metal, but improving performances from Tomjanovich and Murphy kept the team competitive, and in 1974–75, the duo led the Rockets to their first playoff berth since relocating to Houston. In the first round of the postseason, Houston shocked the favored New York Knicks in a three-game series. However, the Rockets were then outclassed in the second round by a talented Boston Celtics team.

CALVIN MURPHY

Simply put, Calvin Murphy was small. His early ambitions were also small. Looking back on his career, Murphy recalled, "My only dream was that I wanted to start for my high school basketball team, the Norwalk High School Bears." Ultimately, Murphy made up for his short stature with big talent. Although he was usually the smallest player on the court in any game, Murphy was also one of the quickest. This quickness made him a sticky defender and a shifty scorer. Murphy also had a high-arcing shot that drove would-be shot blockers crazy as it soared over them with pinpoint accuracy. When Murphy didn't have his view obstructed by taller players, he made the most of it. The point guard set NBA records for consecutive free throws made (78) and free throw percentage (.958) during the 1980–81 season. The longtime Rockets standout also represented stable leadership for the franchise. Murphy was inducted into the Basketball Hall of Fame in 1993. Afterward, one of his former high school coaches joked, "Yeah, I reckon he was good enough to make our team."

SEEKING THE PROMISED LAND

MOSES MALONE WAS THE FIRST PLAYER EVER TO GO PRO STRAIGHT OUT OF HIGH SCHOOL.

To move up another rung on the NBA ladder, the Rockets put their hopes in center Moses Malone. Malone had professional experience in the American Basketball Association (ABA), and the Rockets became his second NBA team (after he played a mere two games for the Buffalo Braves) when he joined them via trade during the 1976–77 season. A bruising player, "Mo" Malone gave Houston the potent scorer and rebounder it had been lacking since Hayes's departure. Also new to Houston that season was rookie guard John Lucas, who provided confident ball-handling and stability. "John doesn't overwhelm you with talent," said Rockets guard Mike Newlin. "He's just smooth. He asserts himself without infringing on anyone else's space, which is really an art."

This bolstered lineup earned the franchise's first winning

ROBERT REID

POSITION GUARD / FORWARD
HEIGHT 6-FOOT-8
ROCKETS SEASONS
1977–82, 1983–88

Robert Reid's stats weren't always overwhelming, but numbers didn't tell his whole story. A dogged defender, Reid was often charged with covering the opposing team's top scorer. In Houston's surprising 1981 playoff run, Reid averaged more than one block and two steals per game while defending star players such as guard Magic Johnson and forward Larry Bird. After taking the 1982–83 season off to focus on religious ministry, Reid returned to provide leadership and stability to a young Houston roster. Late in the 1985–86 season, an injury left the Rockets without a point guard. Reid shifted from backup guard/forward to starting point guard and proceeded to guide the Rockets all the way to the NBA Finals. Throughout his successes, Reid remained humble. Following a game in which he tallied 19 points and 10 offensive rebounds while holding Larry Bird to 8 points, reporters wondered if there was some secret to the performance. Reid told them, "I got up this morning, ate some Froot Loops, watched Tarzan save Boy from an alligator on television, and came down here to take my warm-ups."

record at 49–33. After a first-round bye in the playoffs, Houston surged past the Hayes-led Bullets. In the Eastern Conference finals, the Rockets played six tough games against the Philadelphia 76ers. However, at the end of a tight Game 6, a controversial charging call against Lucas ended Houston's hopes of an NBA Finals appearance.

The Rockets seemed poised to go a step farther the next year before a frightening incident derailed them. During a midseason game against the Los Angeles Lakers, a fight broke out, and hulking Lakers forward Kermit Washington hit Tomjanovich in the face with a devastating punch that ended his season. Without Tomjanovich's scoring and leadership, Houston finished 28–54.

In 1978–79, Tomjanovich was back, and Malone enjoyed perhaps his finest season. The hardworking center averaged 24.8 points and 17.6 rebounds a game to earn the NBA Most Valuable Player (MVP) award. Unfortunately, Houston fell to the Atlanta Hawks in the first round of the playoffs. The Rockets fared only marginally better the following postseason, reaching the second round before being swept by the Celtics.

The Rockets went a mediocre 40–42 in 1980–81 but sneaked into the playoffs. Once there, they stunned the league by defeating three favored opponents to reach the NBA Finals. Few fans or experts gave Houston any chance against star forward Larry Bird and the Celtics, but the Rockets—behind Malone, Murphy, and swingman Robert Reid—won two games before their unlikely run was ended in Game 6. "Every member of our team can take great pride in playing on a team that people said wouldn't win a single playoff game," said Houston head coach Del Harris.

Over the next couple of years, many of Houston's familiar faces disappeared. Tomjanovich retired before the 1981–82 season, and Murphy's playing time dropped. Despite another MVP season from Malone, the Rockets were bounced from the playoffs in round one. Afterward, Houston decided to trade Malone to the 76ers for mediocre center Caldwell Jones and a future draft pick. This left a gaping hole in the Houston frontcourt, and in 1982–83, the Rockets fell to an embarrassing 14–68. It seemed the Rockets had run out of fuel.

ROBERT HORRY

CHOKE CITY TO CLUTCH CITY

"Choke City." This was the new nickname for Houston suggested in a newspaper headline following the Rockets' back-to-back collapses in round two of the 1994 playoffs. In Game 1 against the Phoenix Suns, Houston let an 18-point lead slip away. It did one better (or worse) in Game 2, wasting a 20-point lead in the fourth quarter. Both losses were on the Rockets' home court, and hopes were rapidly fading. "We traveled directly to Phoenix after the game," center Hakeem Olajuwon said. "That was a terrible flight. It was silent on the plane, as if somebody had died. Nobody was prepared for what had happened." In Game 3, the Rockets were trailing by eight at halftime. However, it was Houston's turn for a comeback, and the Rockets crushed the Suns in the second half. Another step-up performance then clinched Game 4 for Houston. Having evened the series in Phoenix, the Rockets returned home to a city with a new nickname: "Clutch City." The Rockets cemented that label by not only winning the Phoenix series but by going on to victory in the NBA Finals as well.

HOUSTON'S TWIN TOWERS

RALPH SAMPSON AND HAKEEM OLAJUWON TOWERED OVER THE COMPETITION.

Houston used the first overall pick in the 1983 NBA Draft to take center Ralph Sampson, a three-time College Player of the Year from the University of Virginia. The team also landed talented forward Rodney McCray. The 7-foot-4 Sampson averaged 21 points, 11.1 rebounds, and 2.4 blocks per game in 1983–84 to earn Rookie of the Year honors. Along with McCray, he boosted the Rockets to 29–53—a significant improvement, but still among the worst records in the NBA. The Rockets won a coin toss to secure the first choice in the 1984 Draft, and with it, they selected another seven-footer—center Akeem (later Hakeem) "The Dream" Olajuwon.

The imposing frontcourt duo of Olajuwon and Sampson, quickly nicknamed the "Twin Towers," not only posted impressive scoring and rebounding numbers but chased

FROM SHADOW TO SPOTLIGHT

One of the most famous shots in Rockets history came from an unexpected source. In the second round of the 1995 playoffs, Houston was down three games to one versus the Phoenix Suns and on the verge of elimination. Some members of that Suns team were still bitter about Houston's round-two series comeback the previous year and publicly promised it wouldn't happen again. Despite such guarantees, the Rockets evened the series by winning Games 5 and 6. Then, in Game 7, the Rockets and Suns were tied in the closing moments, and Houston guard Mario Elie had the ball. The journeyman Elie had played for four teams in his six NBA seasons, typically coming off the bench. Everyone in Phoenix's America West Arena expected him to pass the ball to star center Hakeem Olajuwon. "Dream was wide-open, but I had my feet set," Elie said. "I let it go, and it felt good." The three-pointer rained through the net with 7.1 seconds remaining, Elie blew the Suns' bench a goodbye kiss, and the Rockets won 115–114 and went on to capture the NBA title.

opposing offenses out of the paint with their shot-blocking prowess. Many thought the Rockets were crazy to stockpile two great players in the same position, putting a combined 14 feet, 4 inches of center on the court each night. Houston coach Bill Fitch disagreed. "I don't know a coach who would tell you that Olajuwon and Sampson can't play together in the same lineup," Fitch said. "Then again, we could cut them in half and make four guards."

In 1985–86, Sampson and Olajuwon, backed by McCray, Lucas, and efficient guard Lewis Lloyd, soared to a 51–31 mark and blasted into the playoffs. In the Western Conference finals, Houston had the mighty Lakers on the ropes, leading the series three games to one. In Game 5, with the score tied 112–112 and one second on the clock, McCray hurled an inbound pass from mid-court. Sampson leaped to catch the pass and, still hanging in the air, lobbed the ball toward the basket 12 feet away. The shot arced over Lakers center Kareem Abdul-Jabbar, bounced high off the rim, and rattled in to clinch the Rockets' spot in the NBA Finals. Unfortunately, the Celtics—who reigned as a powerhouse throughout the '80s—then

AT 7-FOOT-1, CENTER TREE ROLLINS CARRIED ON HOUSTON'S TRADITION OF BIG MEN IN THE PAINT.

COURTSIDE STORIES
A CHAMPIONSHIP OVERDUE

For two years straight in the early 1980s, the University of Houston Cougars lost in college basketball's national championship game. That highflying, dunk-happy squad—affectionately known as "Phi Slamma Jamma"— included center Akeem "The Dream" Olajuwon and guard Clyde "The Glide" Drexler. In the NBA, both players quickly emerged as stars, though championships still eluded them. With their respective NBA teams—Olajuwon in Houston and Drexler in Portland—each player experienced runner-up seasons as they had in college, being bested in the NBA Finals by the likes of the Boston Celtics, Detroit Pistons, and Chicago Bulls. Then Olajuwon's Rockets won the 1994 NBA championship, and late in the 1994–95 season, Houston traded with the Trail Blazers to bring Drexler back "home." The duo of Olajuwon and Drexler powered the Rockets through the playoffs and to a four-game sweep of the Magic in the 1995 Finals to at last give the reunited teammates a championship season together. "It was great to win the championship in the place where it all began," said Drexler.

"OLAJUWON IS BLESSED WITH GRACE, ABILITY, AND QUICKNESS. . . . HIS EDGE IS HIS ABILITY TO OUTDO HIS OPPONENTS PHYSICALLY: OUTJUMP, OUTQUICK, OUTRUN THEM."

— RICK BARRY ON HAKEEM OLAJUWON

thwarted the Rockets once again, claiming the trophy in six games.

The Rockets experienced a letdown the following year and broke up the Twin Towers in 1987, by trading Sampson. The still-improving Olajuwon boasted amazing agility and devastating moves in the low post. He attributed much of his crafty footwork to his experience playing soccer while growing up in Nigeria. "Olajuwon is blessed with grace, ability, and quickness . . . ," marveled former Rockets guard Rick Barry. "His edge is his ability to outdo his opponents physically: outjump, outquick, outrun them."

Starting with the 1987–88 campaign, the Rockets enjoyed four more straight playoff seasons, adding muscular power forward Otis Thorpe and quick guards Kenny Smith and Vernon Maxwell along the way. Unfortunately, each postseason ended prematurely, as Houston suffered first-round defeats every time.

In the midst of an unremarkable 1991–92 season, former Rockets star Rudy Tomjanovich took over as interim head coach. Houston hoped that the steady leadership he had provided on the court as a player would carry over to the bench. The Rockets failed to reach the playoffs, but Tomjanovich proved himself capable enough to be named full-time head coach after the season.

In 1992–93, Olajuwon excelled under Tomjanovich, posting his best statistical season yet. Rookie forward Robert Horry—a rangy defender with an accurate shooting touch—added versatility and immediately cracked the starting lineup. Following a 55-win regular season, Houston won its first postseason series in 6 years. The Rockets' second-round matchup with the Seattle SuperSonics was an evenly waged battle that culminated in a Game 7 overtime. The Rockets were edged out, 103–100, but they aspired to go higher yet. "It's tough losing close ones," said Horry, "but it shows how close we are."

HAKEEM OLAJUWON

POSITION CENTER
HEIGHT 7 FEET
ROCKETS SEASONS
1984–2001

A humble and gentle man off the court, Hakeem "The Dream" Olajuwon was a nightmare for opposing teams on the hardwood. Although the Nigerian center had never played organized basketball until he was a high school senior, he was soon routinely swatting shots on one end of the court, and then dazzling fans and frustrating defenders with his agile moves and deft shooting touch on the other end. Olajuwon developed a set of offensive fakes and spins that was so difficult to defend it was given its own name—the Dream Shake. The Dream Shake was unpredictable and nearly indefensible, capped off by a variety of lay-ins, fadeaways, or hook shots. Fellow NBA center Shaquille O'Neal calculated, "Hakeem has five moves, then four countermoves. That gives him 20 moves." The pinnacle of Olajuwon's career came in 1993–94, when he led the Rockets to an NBA championship and was named both NBA MVP and Defensive Player of the Year. When he retired in 2002, Olajuwon was the only player in NBA history to rank in the top 10 in career scoring, rebounding, blocked shots, and steals.

THE ROCKETS
BLAST OFF

IN THE 1994 PLAYOFFS, OTIS THORPE SNAGGED AN AVERAGE OF 9.9 REBOUNDS PER GAME.

In 1993, the Chicago Bulls' era of domination temporarily ended with the short-lived retirement of superstar guard Michael Jordan. The championship trophy now stood vulnerable, and the timing worked out perfectly for the Rockets. Tomjanovich's starting five remained intact from the previous season, and Olajuwon was at the peak of his career. In 1993–94, he averaged 27.3 points, 11.9 boards, and 3.7 blocks per game, earning both the league MVP and Defensive Player of the Year awards. Houston soared to win both the Midwest Division and the second seed in the Western Conference playoffs.

In the postseason, the Rockets navigated a gauntlet of talented and experienced opponents—the Portland Trail Blazers, Phoenix Suns, and Utah Jazz—to reach the NBA Finals. There they faced the New York Knicks—a team much like their own. The rugged and confident Knicks were

LEARNING FROM THE BEST

When the Rockets acquired rookie center Yao Ming in 2002, he was already a talented player. Still, he was only 22 years old, and the Rockets saw potential for tremendous growth. After Yao's first season, the Rockets brought in Patrick Ewing as an assistant coach. Ewing had assembled a Hall of Fame career playing center for New York. In fact, it was Ewing and his Knicks whom the Rockets had narrowly defeated in the 1994 NBA Finals. Houston was eager to have him contribute to the development of young Yao. The following year, Houston added veteran Dikembe Mutombo to the roster. "Mount Mutombo" was among the greatest defensive centers of all time. He also demonstrated great leadership, work habits, and personal dignity, making him an ideal role model for the maturing Yao. If that wasn't enough, Yao began training with Rockets legend Hakeem Olajuwon, practicing spin moves, drop steps, and jump hooks. Referring to Yao's tutelage under three historic centers, one team official noted, "If he picks up even a fraction of what these guys can teach, the NBA had better watch out."

"WE HAD NONBELIEVERS ALL ALONG THE WAY,
AND I HAVE ONE THING TO SAY TO THOSE
NONBELIEVERS: DON'T EVER UNDERESTIMATE THE
HEART OF A CHAMPION."

— RUDY TOMJANOVICH ON BEING NBA CHAMPS

led by center Patrick Ewing, whose stats and accolades rivaled Olajuwon's. And like Olajuwon, Ewing had a supporting cast of big forwards and aggressive guards.

The Finals proved to be a hard-fought series. Down three games to two, the Rockets held on to win Game 6 by a score of 86–84 when Olajuwon blocked a potential game-winning three-pointer by Knicks guard John Starks. Game 7 was played at Houston's arena, The Summit. In a game in which the usual stars struggled to make shots, Houston's guard trio of Maxwell, Smith, and rookie Sam Cassell combined to hit 14 of 24 field-goal attempts and 13 of 14 free throws. Their efficient contributions helped Houston claim a 90–84 victory and the franchise's first NBA title. "This was a tough battle," said a jubilant Olajuwon. "It was truly a championship game. If you write a book, you can't write it any better."

After waiting 26 years for their first NBA crown, the Rockets were poised to defend it the next season, but their Western Conference opponents were growing ever stronger. Rather than wait for the competition to catch up, the Rockets aimed to stay ahead of the curve. Midway through the season, Houston traded

Thorpe to Portland for All-Star guard Clyde "The Glide" Drexler. Even so, the conference had become so daunting that the Rockets earned only the sixth-best record.

Once the postseason began, Houston showed its mettle. Olajuwon and Drexler consistently gave impressive performances, but even so, the Rockets would have been grounded had it not been for clutch shots by Horry, Smith, Cassell, and guard Mario Elie. Houston's team efforts spurred it past the West's top three teams to return to the NBA Finals. There, the Rockets took on the Orlando Magic, who featured enormous center Shaquille O'Neal and swift guard Penny Hardaway. But the more experienced Rockets outplayed the young squad, and Houston swept the series to repeat as champions. Afterward, Tomjanovich said, "We had nonbelievers all along the way, and I have one thing to say to those nonbelievers: Don't ever underestimate the heart of a champion."

After falling short in the 1996 playoffs, the Rockets traded away four players for burly

RUDY TOMJANOVICH

POSITION FORWARD, COACH
HEIGHT 6-FOOT-8
ROCKETS SEASONS AS
PLAYER 1970–81, AS
COACH 1992–2003

Rudy Tomjanovich was one of the Rockets' first stars. His most noticeable skill was his accurate shooting, as he knocked down more than 50 percent of his shots during his career. "Rudy T" also was a smart ball handler and could be a tough rebounder. This versatility earned him five All-Star Game selections. Tomjanovich had a great understanding of the game and a willingness to do whatever was needed—characteristics that translated well to his coaching career. But he was actually reluctant to become a head coach. "I really loved being an assistant coach," he said. "I didn't want the spotlight." Once he took up that post, though, Tomjanovich worked hard and was well-liked by his players. He could be seen and heard pacing the sidelines, hoarsely shouting instructions to players and arguing with refs. Yet for all his intensity during games, he was modest off the court, accepting blame for the team's failures while giving players the credit for successes. But there was often enough credit to go around. In just his second and third full seasons as head coach, Tomjanovich guided the Rockets to back-to-back NBA championships.

forward Charles Barkley, giving Houston's lineup three future Hall-of-Famers. Barkley helped the 1996–97 Rockets go 57–25 and push as far as the Western Conference finals, but Utah thwarted a return to the championship series. Injuries led to a mediocre season the next year, and Drexler retired. To fill the void, Houston traded for another veteran superstar—Chicago forward Scottie Pippen. The Rockets put together a solid regular season but lost in the first round of the 1999 playoffs. In the 1999–2000 season, a knee injury ended Barkley's career, and age and injuries decreased Olajuwon's effectiveness. Without these perennial All-Stars leading the way, the Rockets' impressive run came to an end, and they missed the playoffs for the first time in eight years.

AFTER THEIR LATE '90s DOWNTURN, THE ROCKETS MOVED TO THE TOYOTA CENTER IN 2003.

OLAJUWON WAS KNOWN
FOR HIS STIFLING PRESENCE
BENEATH THE BASKET.

BACK DOWN
TO EARTH

CUTTINO "CAT" MOBLEY STARED DOWN OPPONENTS, LOOKING FOR CHANCES TO SCORE.

The next few seasons were uncharacteristic for the Rockets. For the first time in club history, Houston ran a guard-oriented offense behind explosive point guard Steve Francis and rapid-fire shooting guard Cuttino Mobley. The duo was fast, enthusiastic, and entertaining, but as Houston became increasingly one-dimensional, it found wins harder to come by. By the end of the 2001–02 campaign, the Rockets ranked among the league's worst defenses and finished with a 28–54 record.

Fortunately, the Rockets' lackluster performance once again helped them land the top overall pick in the 2002 NBA Draft. Hoping to bring back the days of a dominating post presence, Houston selected 7-foot-6 center Yao Ming from Shanghai, China. Yao's rookie numbers weren't miraculous, but his presence on the court helped keep

opposing offenses out of the paint while bringing more balance to Houston's offense. The Rockets finished the season back above .500, and their enormous new center was only getting better. "It will take time to adapt," said Yao on learning the NBA game, "but I think I can handle it."

Houston fans were amped up about the team's prospects heading into the 2003–04 campaign. Adding to the sense of hope and change were a new arena, Toyota Center, and new coach Jeff Van Gundy. That season, an improved Yao and the Rockets reached the playoffs for the first time in five years.

Expectations were heightened the following off-season, as Houston dealt Francis and Mobley to Orlando for forward Tracy McGrady. "T-Mac" boasted a rare combination of size (6-foot-8), shooting ability, quickness, and ball-handling

skills that had made him the NBA's top scorer the previous two seasons. But equally important to the Rockets were his other contributions. In 2004–05, McGrady led the team in assists and steals, ranked second in rebounding, and came in third in blocks. Behind the potent one-two punch of McGrady and Yao, the Rockets won 51 games and took the Dallas Mavericks to 7 games in the opening round of the playoffs. Although it was dealt a crushing blow in Game 7, losing by 40 points, Houston remained confident in its future prospects. "It was really not befitting how we played and conducted ourselves this year," said Van Gundy following the blowout loss. "The way it ended does not reflect well on myself or the team, but it does not affect my overall pride."

Unfortunately, just as the Rockets seemed to be on the rise, Yao and McGrady missed a

YAO MING

**POSITION CENTER
HEIGHT 7-FOOT-6
ROCKETS SEASONS
2002–11**

When the Rockets selected Yao Ming from China with the first pick in the 2002 NBA Draft, they acquired a giant. Even among other NBA centers, Yao was often a half foot taller and 50 pounds heavier than anyone else on the court. He performed the tasks expected of such a huge man—challenging opponents' shots and hauling in rebounds—but it was his polished offensive ability that separated Yao from other seven-foot-plus centers. Considering his size, Yao developed impressive footwork and body control, allowing him to get good position under the basket and keep defenders off balance. An accurate shooter, he consistently made more than 50 percent of his shots from the floor and better than 80 percent of his free throws. Basketball skills aside, Yao had a positive and caring outlook on life, as coach Rudy Tomjanovich quickly noticed. "He has leadership qualities, and he's a guy that sets a fantastic image and example for people," Tomjanovich said. "I think when you find a player that has talent and that type of personality, the combination is truly something."

41

TRACY McGRADY WAS ALREADY A LEGEND BY THE TIME HE TIPPED THE BALL IN HOUSTON.

LUIS SCOLA

COURTSIDE STORIES
CREATING BRAND AWARENESS

Aside from having a dominant team, a sure-fire way to pack in a crowd is to have fan-friendly players. In the 2012 off-season, Houston spiced up its ho-hum squad by adding James Harden, Jeremy Lin, and Omer Asik. Harden was an explosive scorer who had just helped the Oklahoma City Thunder reach the NBA Finals, but he was perhaps better known for his Mohawk hairstyle and bushy beard. Meanwhile, Lin had just come off a rags-to-riches season in New York: after Knicks stars became sidelined by injuries, the scarcely used point guard was thrust into the starting lineup. Over a 12-game stretch, Lin averaged 22.5 points and 8.7 assists, drained a game-winning three-pointer, and led the hobbled Knicks to 9 victories, sparking nationwide interest that was dubbed "Linsanity." Asik was a Turkish-born seven-footer who may not have commanded as much national attention, but his penchant for rejections, his two-handed jams punctuated by splayed leg lifts, and memorable nicknames such as "The Turkish Hammer" and "Asik and Destroy" cemented his status as a local favorite.

combined 60 games, and the Rockets sputtered in 2005–06. The two stars were sidelined much of the following season as well, but usually one or the other was able to suit up and lead the charge each game, each averaging about 25 points per contest when healthy. The Rockets posted a solid 52–30 record in the regular season before suffering another disappointing Game 7 loss (this time to Utah) in a first-round playoff clash.

The injury bug again plagued Yao and McGrady the following season. But new head coach Rick Adelman maintained high standards for a supporting cast that included shifty point guard Rafer Alston, savvy forward Shane Battier, and rookie forwards Luis Scola and Carl Landry. A full-team effort propelled the Rockets to 55 wins, but they quickly fizzled out in a postseason matchup against Utah for the second straight year. Despite Houston's string of first-round failures, the Rockets still believed they were on the rise. "[We've got] a bunch of young guys that have a bright future," McGrady said.

In 2008–09, the development of two such youngsters—Scola and speedy second-year point guard Aaron Brooks—helped the Rockets finish 53–29 and make it over the first-round playoff hump by beating the Trail Blazers. Unfortunately, that was to be the peak of success during the Yao/McGrady era. In 2009–10, Yao missed the entire season after having foot surgery, and the injury-prone McGrady was traded to New York in a swap that brought high-scoring guard Kevin Martin to town. The Rockets finished just 42–40 and out of playoff

contention. Yao would play just five games the following season before calling an end to his career. After Houston narrowly missed the playoffs yet again, Coach Adelman was replaced by Kevin McHale. The coaching change seemed to have little effect, as Houston remained respectable behind Martin and Scola in 2011–12, but not good enough to reach the postseason.

The Rockets shook things up heading into the 2012–13 season, dismissing or dealing away their top five scorers from the previous season, including Scola and Martin. The revamped roster included the dynamic, young guard tandem of James Harden and Jeremy Lin, plus seven-foot center Omer Asik. Asik topped the league in rebounds (with 956), while Harden was among the scoring leaders. Houston's explosive offense carried it all the way to the playoffs, where it was defeated by the Thunder in the first round.

The following season, Houston found itself within striking distance of the Western Conference title. Harden and center Dwight Howard made for an impressive inside-outside duo, while guard Patrick Beverley and forwards Chandler Parsons and Terrence Jones rounded out the starting lineup.

The Houston area will long be associated with gutsy events that changed the very course of American history, and yet the city continues to strive for further achievements. Likewise, the Houston Rockets have already carved out a proud niche in NBA history but are not content with past glory. Today's Rockets are determined to blast into the future with old-fashioned grit and new-age innovation as they seek to make their next mark on history.

THE DOMINATING
DWIGHT HOWARD
REACHED NEW HEIGHTS
WITH THE ROCKETS.

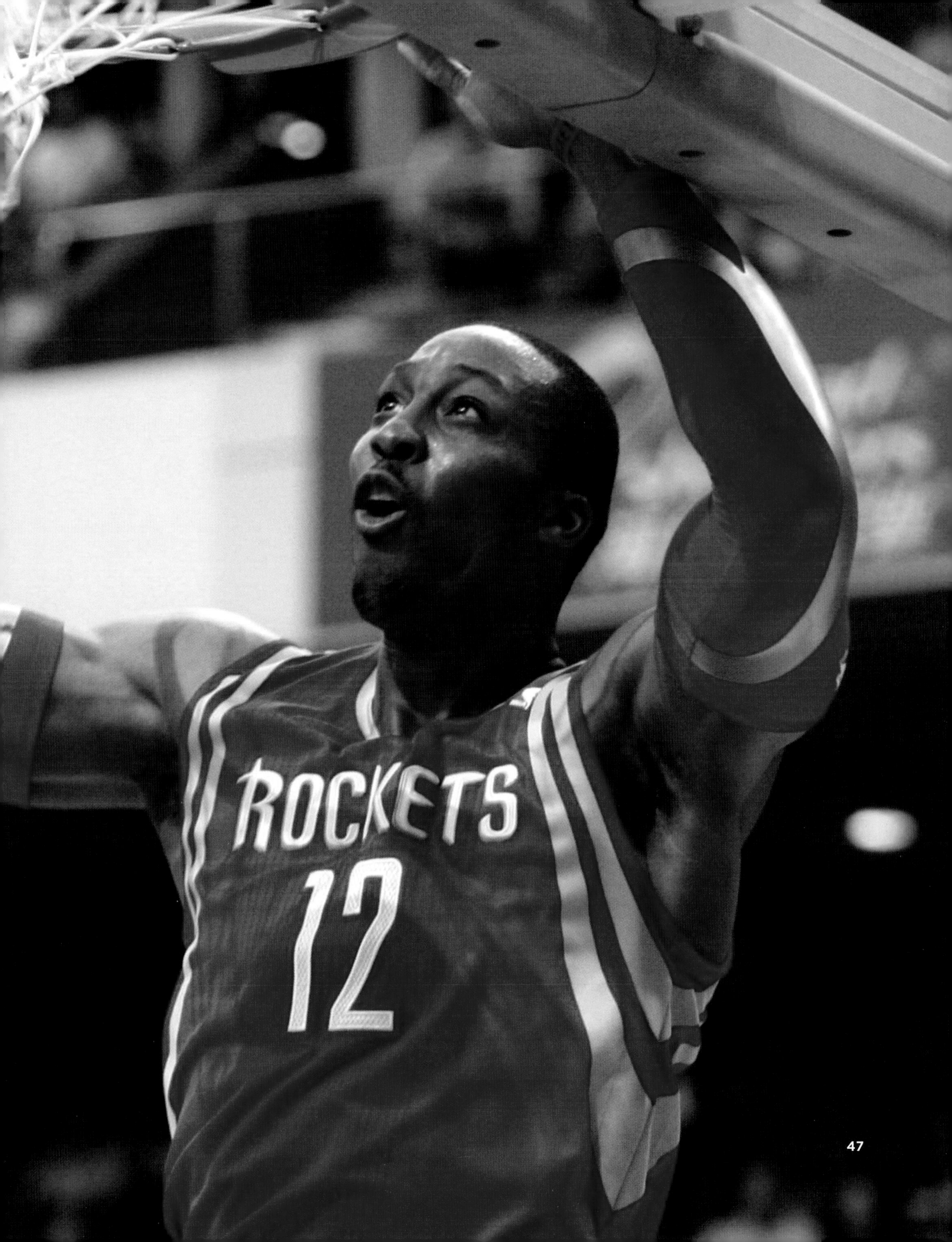
ROCKETS
12

INDEX